Hide and Seek

Jane Thompson and Stephen Thompson

Pupil's Book 1

CB125172

CENGAGE Learning

Australia • Brazil • Mexico • Singapore • United Kingdom • United States

Hide and Seek 1 Scope and sequence

Unit	Topic	Structures	Lexis and phrases	Functions	Alphabet	Numbers	Maths	Our world	Values	Art
1	Hello!	I'm (a) ... This is ... / This isn't ... Is this ... ? She's/He's (a) ... We're/They're ... Yes No There is ...	Hello, boy, girl, teacher, friends, and, Look! Goodbye My name's	Greetings Instructions	a/A, b/B	1, lots Understand 1 as a single object Discriminate between 1 and lots	2D shapes: circle	Sort into groups: boy(s) or girl(s)	Listen to the teacher	Make a bookmark to use in class
2	My body	What's this? It's a/an ... This is my/your ... What's this? It's the robot's (arm). (A spider) has/doesn't have ...	robot, head, legs, arms, hands, feet, body, toes	Identify parts of the body	c/C, d/D	2 3	2D shapes: square	Animals with no legs, 2 legs and lots of legs How animals move (*swim, fly, walk, hop*)	Wash hands	Make a friendship tree
3	Our classroom	There's a ... , There's one ... , There are ... These are ... How many? (Triangles) have ...	classroom, door, window, table (desk), book, chair, board, crayons, pencil, pen, child(ren)	Identify objects Answer questions about numbers	e/E, f/F	4 5	2D shapes: triangle	Properties: big/small animals Heavy /light objects and animals	A tidy classroom	Colour a picture and make a jigsaw puzzle
4	My family	Who's this/that? That's my ... Is it ... ? Yes, it is./No, it isn't. What's his/her name?	family mummy, daddy sister, brother	Identify people Ask and answer questions about people	g/G, h/H	Consolidation of 1-5 Introduce zero, 0	Comparison: tall and small	Animal mothers and babies Families around the world	Help others	Draw and colour a family picture
5	My toys	Where's the ... ? It's here/over there. Where are the ... ? They're here/over there.	toys, ball, bike, bricks, car, plane, blue, red,	Describe and answer questions about location Request and respond politely	i/I, j/J	Sequencing: first, next, before, after	Positional words: here, over there	Hard and soft objects Differentiating between real things and toys	Share toys	Make a ball

Unit	Topic	Structures	Lexis and phrases	Functions	Alphabet	Numbers	Maths	Our world	Values	Art
6	Our senses	What can you see? I can see ... Show me something (green). What colour is it?	eyes, ears, green, yellow motorbike, train	Describe physical appearance Ask and answer questions about colour	k/K, l/L	6 7 one more; one less	Straight, curved, wavy and zig-zag lines Sort shapes by properties	Baby and adult animals and their calls Identifying everyday sounds	Be safe outdoors	Make a shaker
7	How are you?	How are you? Are you OK? I'm fine, thank you. Are you well? Oh dear! I'm sorry. That's nice. Oh, good!	happy, sad, ill, well, fine, very, new, today	Ask and answer about emotional states	m/M, n/N	8 9 Counting on	2D shapes: rectangle Same or different?	Hot and cold Investigate how materials can change (melting and freezing)	Be a good friend	Make a card
8	Weather	What's the weather like? Is the weather nice? It's (sunny).	hot, cold wet, sunny, cloudy, windy, good, bad	Ask and answer questions about the weather	o/O, p/P, q/Q, r/R	10	Sorting common objects	Seasons Water evaporation	Save water	Make a windsock or a fan
9	Our pets	What's that? Be careful! Don't touch! Don't hurt them! Feed the ... Always give ...	pet, bird, cat, rabbit, fish animal	Give positive and negative instructions	s/S, t/T, u/U, v/V	Consolidation of numbers 0-5; identifying one more and one less	Positional words: in, on, under	Distinguish fur, feathers and scales Using a magnifying glass	Care for pets	Paint a symmetrical butterfly
10	Day and night	Everyone is (asleep). It's noisy/quiet, (There are) lots of cars. What can you see (in the daytime)?	light, dark, bright day(time), night(time), sun, star moon, rain, rainbow, shadow	Describe physical appearance and times of day	w/W, x/X, y/Y, z/Z	Review numbers 0-10	Identify common 2D shapes within larger images; Describe the properties of 2D shapes	Rainbows Shadows	Good bedtime behaviour	Make a starry night picture

Unit 1 • Lesson 1

Hello!

Key language:
Hello; Miss Hill; Sam; Tarik, Lin; Dona; yes; no; goodbye

- Warm up
- Hide and seek: *a* **1.2**
- Rhyme: *Hello!* **1.3**
- Look, listen and say. **1.4**
- Game: *Hello!*
- Rhyme: *Goodbye* **1.5**

a

a b c d e f g h i j k l m

1

2

Unit 1 • Lesson 2
Friends

Key language:
I'm ... ; we're friends

- Warm up
- Hide and seek: *b* **1.6**
- Rhyme: *Alphabet* [to *a, b*] **1.7**
- Listen, point and say. **1.8**
- Game: *Introductions*
- Rhyme: *Goodbye* **1.5**

b

n o p q r s t u v w x y z

Unit 1 • Lesson 3

Circles

Key language:
circle; This is/isn't a ... ;
Is this a ... ?

- Warm up
- Hide and seek: *1* **1.9**
- Rhyme: *Numbers* [*1*] **1.10**
- Look, point and say.
- Game: *Match the shape.*
- Rhyme: *Goodbye* **1.5**

1 2 3 4 5

Unit 1 · Lesson 4

One and lots

Key language: *lots; lots of*

- Warm up
- Numbers: *1* and *lots*
- Rhyme: *Numbers* [*1*] **1.10**
- Look and circle.
- Game: *Lots of circles*
- Rhyme: *Goodbye* **1.5**

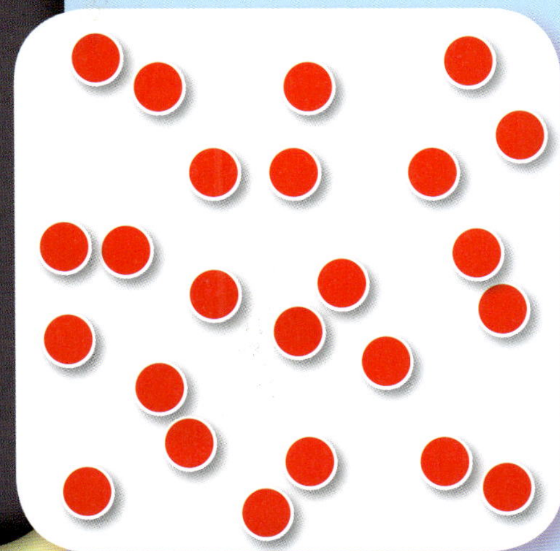

6 7 8 9 10

Unit 1 • Lesson 5

Boy or girl?

Key language:
boy; girl; He's/She's a ... ; (Name's) a ... ; Is he/she a ... ?

- Warm up
- Letters and numbers
- Rhyme: *Our world* 1.11
- Listen, say and draw.
- Game: *Who is it?*
- Rhyme: *Goodbye* 1.5

1

2

Unit 1 • Lesson 6

Boys and girls

Key language:

boys; girls; They're boys/girls; (Name) and (Name) are boys; Are they ... ?

- Warm up
- Letters and numbers
- Rhyme: *Our world* **1.11**
- Look, listen and stick.
- Game: *Boys and girls*
- Rhyme: *Come and play!* **1.12**

Unit 1 • Lesson 7

Listen to the teacher

Key language:
good listening

- Warm up
- Letters and numbers
- Rhyme: *Values* **1.13**
- Point and stick.
- Game: *Choose*
- Rhyme: *Goodbye* **1.5**

I can listen.

Unit 1 • Lesson 8

Make a bookmark

1

2

3

4

Key language:
bookmark; colour (v); stick; pen; neatly

- Warm up
- Letters and numbers
- Rhyme: *Art* 1.14
- Look, listen and make.
- Game: *Boys and girls*
- Rhyme: *Goodbye* 1.5

Unit 2 • Lesson 1

Arms and legs

Key language:
This is my arm/leg/head; It's a/an ... ; It isn't a/an ... ; What's this? robot

- Warm up
- Hide and seek: *c* **1.15**
- Rhyme: *Choose*
- Listen, point and say. **1.16**
- Game: *Robots*
- Rhyme: *Goodbye* **1.5**

c

a b c d e f g h i j k l m

Unit 2 • Lesson 2

My robot

Key language:
head; body; It's the robot's ... ; Is this (Name's) ... ?

- Warm up
- Hide and seek: *d* **1.17**
- Rhyme: *My body (V1)* **1.18**
- Listen, point and say. **1.19**
- Game: *Robot says*
- Rhyme: *Alphabet* [to *c, d*] **1.20**

n o p q r s t u v w x y z

Unit 2 • Lesson 3

Squares

Key language:
two; square

- Warm up
- Hide and seek: *2* 1.21
- Rhyme: *Numbers* [to *2*] 1.22
- Look, listen and find.
- Game: *Circles and squares*
- Rhyme: *Goodbye* 1.5

1 2 3 4 5

Unit 2 · Lesson 4

2 and 3

Key language:
three

- Warm up
- Hide and seek: *3* **1.23**
- Rhyme: *Numbers* [to *3*] **1.24**
- Look and point.
- Game: *Shapes*
- Rhyme: *Goodbye* **1.5**

6 7 8 9 10

Unit 2 • Lesson 5

Hands and feet

Key language:
hands; feet; ... has/doesn't have ... ; snake; monkey; spider

- Warm up
- Letters and numbers
- Rhyme: *Our world* 1.11
- Look and draw.
- Game: *Robot says*
- Rhyme: *My body (V1)* 1.18

Unit 2 · Lesson 6

Fish, birds and kangaroos

Key language:
swim; fly; hop; walk; run; stop; fish; birds; kangaroos

- Warm up
- Letters and numbers
- Rhyme: *My body (V1–2)* **1.25**
- Look, point and stick.
- Game: *Move and stop!*
- Rhyme: *Fish swim* **1.26**

Unit 2 • Lesson 7

Wash your hands

Key language:
wash (your hands); dirty

- Warm up
- Letters and numbers
- Rhyme: *Values* **1.13**
- Look, listen and say.
- Game: *Choose*
- Rhyme: *Wash* **1.27**

I know when to wash my hands.

Unit 2 · Lesson 8

Friendship tree

Key language:
paper; draw; decorate

- Warm up
- Letters and numbers
- Rhyme: *Art* 1.14
- Look, listen and make.
- Game: *Choose*
- Rhyme: *Goodbye* 1.5

Unit 3 • Lesson 1

Our classroom

Key language: *classroom; door; window; board*

- Warm up
- Hide and seek: *e* **1.28**
- Rhyme: My body (*V1–2*) **1.25**
- Listen, point and say. **1.29**
- Game: *Come and go!*
- Rhyme: *Goodbye* **1.5**

e

a b c d e f g h i j k l m

Unit 3 · Lesson 2

Tables and chairs

Key language: *There are … ; teacher; child; children; chair; table*

- Warm up
- Hide and seek: *f* **1.30**
- Rhyme: *Alphabet* [to *e, f*] **1.31**
- Listen, point and say. **1.32**
- Game: *Show me 1, 2, 3.*
- Rhyme: *Come and play!* **1.12**

f

n o p q r s t u v w x y z

Unit 3 • Lesson 3

Triangles

Key language:
four; triangle; side

- Warm up
- Hide and seek: 4 **1.33**
- Rhyme: *One, two. How are you?* [to 4] **1.34**
- Look, listen and find.
- Game: *Shapes*
- Rhyme: *Numbers* [to 4] **1.35**

1 2 3 4 5

Unit 3 • Lesson 4
How many?

Key language:
five; Tell me; How many?; fingers

- Warm up
- Hide and seek: *5* **1.36**
- Rhyme: *Numbers* [to *5*]
- Count and match.
- Game: *Cloud game*
- Rhyme: *Shamlar the camel* **1.38**

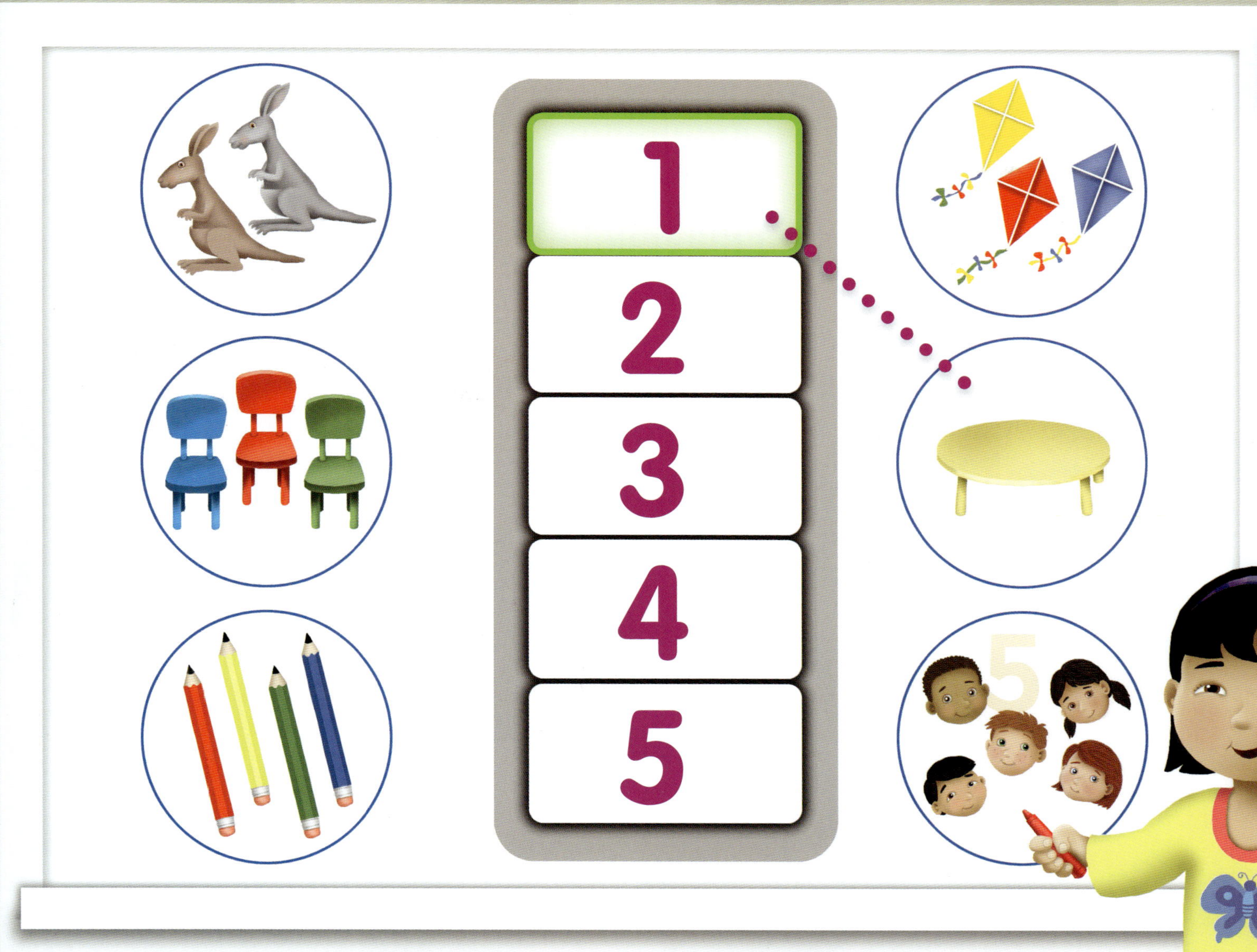

6 7 8 9 10

Unit 3 · Lesson 5

Big and small

Key language:
big; small; These are …

- Warm up
- Letters and numbers
- Rhyme: *Our world* 1.11
- Look and say.
- Game: *Make big and small.*
- Rhyme: *My body (V1–2)* 1.25

Unit 3 · Lesson 6

Heavy and light

Key language:
heavy; light

- Warm up
- Letters and numbers
- Rhyme: *Our world* **1.11**
- Say and stick.
- Game: *Heavy or light?*
- Rhyme: *Fish swim* **1.26**

Unit 3 • Lesson 7
A tidy room

Key language:
tidy; untidy; rubbish; bin; pot; box; put

- Warm up
- Letters and numbers
- Rhyme: *Values* **1.13**
- Look, listen and say.
- Game: *Pairs*
- Rhyme: *Wash* **1.27**

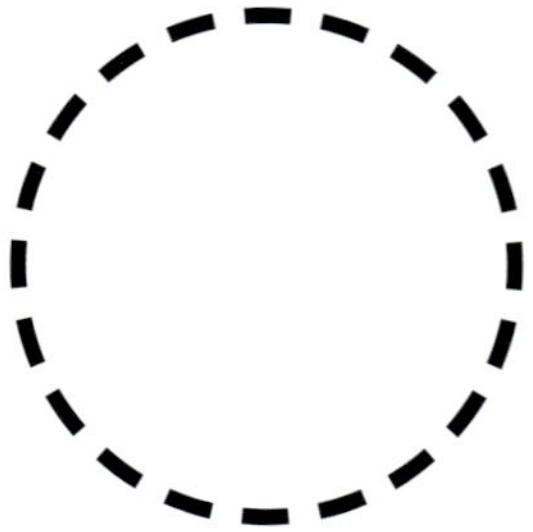

I am tidy.

Unit 3 • Lesson 8

Jigsaw fun

Key language:
red; blue; pen(s); crayon(s)

- Warm up
- Letters and numbers
- Rhyme: *Art* 1.14
- Colour and play.
- Game: *Choose*
- Rhyme: *Goodbye* 1.5

1

2

3

4

Unit 4 • Lesson 1

My family

Key language:
My brother; daddy; family; That's (my) ... ; His name's ...

- Warm up
- Hide and seek: *g* **1.39**
- Rhyme: *Choose*
- Listen, point and say. **1.40**
- Game: *Come and go!*
- Rhyme: *Goodbye* **1.5**

g

a b c d e f g h i j k l m

1

2

Unit 4 • Lesson 2

Brothers and sisters

Key language:
mummy; sister; Who's that?; That's (my) ... ; Her name's ...

- Warm up
- Hide and seek: *h* **1.41**
- Rhyme: *Choose*
- Listen, point and say. **1.42**
- Game: *Snap!*
- Rhyme: *Alphabet* [to *g, h*] **1.43**

h

n o p q r s t u v w x y z

Unit 4 • Lesson 3
Zero

Key language:
zero; no (balloons); flowers

- Warm up
- Hide and seek: *0* **1.44**
- Rhyme: *Shamlar the camel* **1.38**
- Look and count to *5.*
- Game: *Groups*
- Rhyme: *There is one fish.* **1.45**

0 1 2 3 4 5

Unit 4 • Lesson 4
Small and tall

Key language: *yellow; tall; (S)He's ... ; It's (tall)*

- Warm up
- Hide and seek: *Shapes*
- Rhyme: *Numbers* [to *5*] **1.37**
- Look, point and say.
- Game: *Big, tall, small*
- Rhyme: *There is one fish.* **1.45**

6 7 8 9 10

Unit 4 • Lesson 5

Baby animals

Key language:
animal; baby; This/That is a ...

- Warm up
- Letters and numbers
- Rhyme: *Our world* **1.11**
- Find and draw.
- Game: *Sounds* **1.46–1.47**
- Rhyme: *Goodbye* **1.5**

Unit 4 · Lesson 6

Parents and children

Key language:
parents

- Warm up
- Letters and numbers
- Rhyme: *Our world* **1.11**
- Look and say.
- Game: *Happy families*
- Rhyme: *My family* **1.48**

Unit 4 • Lesson 7

Let's help others

Key language:
pick (things) up; put (things) away; please

- Warm up
- Letters and numbers
- Rhyme: *Values* 1.13
- Say and draw.
- Game: *Help at home.*
- Rhyme: *Helping others* 1.49

I help at home.

Unit 4 · Lesson 8

Me and my family

Key language:
grown-up

- Warm up
- Letters and numbers
- Rhyme: *Art* **1.14**
- Listen and draw.
- Game: *Choose*
- Rhyme: *Goodbye* **1.5**

1

2

3

4

Unit 5 • Lesson 1

My toys

Key language:
Where's the ... ; toys; here; It's over there; bike; plane

- Warm up
- Hide and seek: *i* 1.50
- Rhyme: *Hello!* 1.3
- Look, listen and say. 1.51
- Game: *Come and go!*
- Rhyme: *Goodbye* 1.5

a b c d e f g h i j k l m

Unit 5 · Lesson 2

Where are the bricks?

Key language: *Where are the … ?; They're … ; bricks; cars; bring*

- Warm up
- Hide and seek: *j* **1.52**
- Rhyme: *Alphabet* [to *i, j*] **1.53**
- Listen, point and say. **1.54**
- Game: *Bring and take!*
- Rhyme: *Come and play!* **1.12**

j

n o p q r s t u v w x y z

Unit 5 • Lesson 3

First, next …

Key language:
first; next; before; after

- Warm up
- Numbers: *First, next*
- Rhyme: *Shamlar the camel* **1.38**
- Listen, point and say.
- Game: *Put in order.*
- Rhyme: *One, two. How are you?* [to 4] **1.34**

0 1 2 3 4 5

Unit 5 · Lesson 4

Where is ... ?

Key language:
duck; box; floor; on; in

- Warm up
- Numbers: *1* to *5*
- Rhyme: *Five baby ducks* **1.55**
- Look, listen and stick. **1.56**
- Game: *Where?*
- Rhyme: *Numbers* [to *5*] **1.37**

6 7 8 9 10

Unit 5 · Lesson 5

Soft and hard

Key language:
hard; soft; house

- Warm up
- Letters and numbers
- Rhyme: *Our world* 1.11
- Look, say and draw.
- Game: *Soft* or *hard?*
- Rhyme: *My body* (*V1–2*) 1.25

Unit 5 • Lesson 6

Real or toy?

Key language:
real or toy?

- Warm up
- Letters and numbers
- Rhyme: *Our world* **1.11**
- Find and circle.
- Game: *Real or toy?*
- Rhyme: *Alphabet* [to *i, j*] **1.53**

Unit 5 • Lesson 7

Sharing

Key language:
sad; happy; Can I share (your) ... ?; car

- Warm up
- Letters and numbers
- Rhyme: *Values* **1.13**
- Look, think and choose.
- Game: *Please and thank you*
- Rhyme: *Wash* **1.27**

I can share.

Unit 5 • Lesson 8

Make a ball

Key language:
wool; string; card; wind (v)

- Warm up
- Letters and numbers
- Rhyme: *Art* 1.14
- Look, listen and make.
- Game: *Catch!*
- Rhyme: *Goodbye* 1.5

1

2

3

4

Unit 6 · Lesson 1

What can you see?

Key language:
eyes; see; What can you see? I can see ... ; green; tractor; Show me something ...

- Warm up
- Hide and seek: *k* **1.57**
- Rhyme: *Choose*
- Look, listen and say. **1.58**
- Game: *Something green*
- Rhyme: *Colours* **1.59**

a b c d e f g h i j k l m

Unit 6 · Lesson 2

Something green!

Key language:
grass; sky; lizard; beetle; What colour is it?

- Warm up
- Hide and seek: *l* **1.60**
- Rhyme: *Colours* **1.59**
- Listen, look and say. **1.61**
- Game: *I can see something!*
- Rhyme: *Alphabet* [to *k*, *l*] **1.62**

l

n o p q r s t u v w x y z

Unit 6 • Lesson 3

Lines

Key language:
six; line; one more

- Warm up
- Numbers: *6* (and *one more*) **1.63**
- Rhyme: *Five baby ducks* **1.55**
- Find and stick.
- Game: *Make lines.*
- Rhyme: *One, two. How are you?* [to *6*] **1.64**

0 1 2 3 4 5

Unit 6 • Lesson 4
Shapes

Key language:
seven; one less; It's (big) and (red).

- Warm up
- Numbers: *7* (and *one less*) **1.65**
- Rhyme: *One, two. How are you?* [to *6*] **1.64**
- Look, listen and stick. **1.66**
- Game: *Shapes*
- Rhyme: *Numbers* [to *7*] **1.67**

6 7 8 9 10

Unit 6 · Lesson 5

I can hear!

Key language:
ears; hear; baby; cat; cow; horse

- Warm up
- Letters and numbers
- Rhyme: *Our world* **1.11**
- Listen and match. **1.68**
- Game: *Where's my Mummy? Where's my Daddy?*
- Rhyme: *Uncle Ali has a farm.* **1.69**

1 2 3 4

Unit 6 · Lesson 6

What can you hear?

Key language:
What can you hear?; motorbike; train

- Warm up
- Letters and numbers
- Rhyme: *Our world* **1.11**
- Look, listen and point. **1.70–1.71**
- Game: *What's that sound?* **1.72**
- Rhyme: *I can hear.* **1.73**

Unit 6 · Lesson 7

Wait, look, listen

Key language:
hold; wait; Stay with ... ; safe; dangerous; always

- Warm up
- Letters and numbers
- Rhyme: *Values* 1.13
- Look, think and choose.
- Game: *Choose*
- Rhyme: *Wait, look, listen.* 1.74

I can be safe outside.

Unit 6 · Lesson 8

Make a shaker

1

2

Key language:
shaker; shake; beans; put in

- Warm up
- Letters and numbers
- Rhyme: *Art* **1.14**
- Look, listen and make.
- Game: *Loud and soft*
- Rhyme: *Goodbye* **1.5**

3

4

Unit 7 · Lesson 1

How are you?

Key language:

How are you? ill; fine;
Are you OK?

- Warm up
- Hide and seek: *m* **2.2**
- Rhyme: *Hello!* **1.3**
- Look, listen and say. **2.3**
- Game: *How are you?*
- Rhyme: *Choose*

m

a b c d e f g h i j k l m

Unit 7 • Lesson 2

I'm happy

Key language: *Are you happy/sad/well? Oh dear!; Oh good!; new; today*

- Warm up
- Hide and seek: *n* **2.4**
- Rhyme: *Alphabet* [to *m, n*] **2.5**
- Look, listen and say. **2.6**
- Game: *Today, I'm ... .*
- Rhyme: *We're happy!* **2.7**

n

n o p q r s t u v w x y z

Unit 7 • Lesson 3

Come for cake!

Key language:
eight; cakes; biscuits

- Warm up
- Hide and seek: *8* **2.8**
- Rhyme: *Numbers* [to *8*] **2.9**
- Find and count.
- Game: *Number fun*
- Rhyme: *One, two. How are you?* [to *8*] **2.10**

8

0 1 2 3 4 5

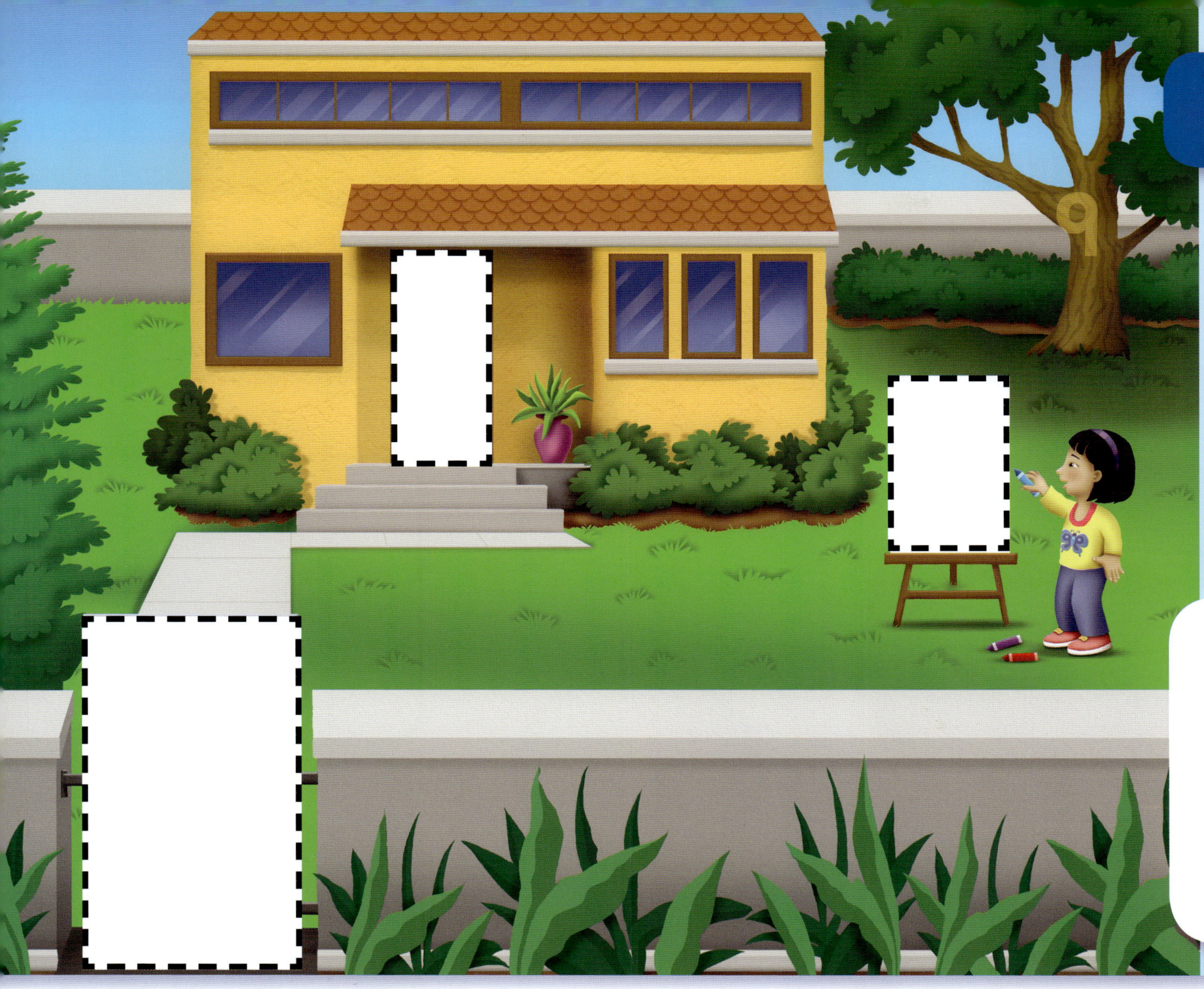

Unit 7 • Lesson 4

Rectangles

Key language:
nine; rectangle; same; different

- Warm up
- Hide and seek: 9 **2.11**
- Rhyme: *Numbers* [to 9] **2.12**
- Look, find and stick.
- Game: *Shapes*
- Rhyme: *Colours* **1.59**

6 7 8 9 10

Unit 7 · Lesson 5

Hot and cold

Key language:
hot; cold; food; drink

- Warm up
- Letters and numbers
- Rhyme: *Our world* 1.11
- Look, point and match.
- Game: *Hot or cold?*
- Rhyme: *Are you cold?* 2.13

1 2 3 4

1 2 3 4

Unit 7 • Lesson 6

Make a lolly

Key language:
ice-cream; yogurt; lolly; cup

- Warm up
- Letters and numbers
- Rhyme: *Our world* 1.11
- Look, listen and number. 2.14
- Make a lolly.
- Rhyme: *Rice and beans* 2.15

1 2 3 4

1 2 3 4

Unit 7 • Lesson 7

Be a good friend

Key language:
card; Get well; Be a good friend

- Warm up
- Letters and numbers
- Rhyme: *Values* **1.13**
- Look, think and draw.
- Game: *Choose*
- Rhyme: *Good friends* **2.16**

I'm a good friend.

Unit 7 • Lesson 8

Make a card

1

2

3

4

Key language:
trace; fold; press

- Warm up
- Letters and numbers
- Rhyme: *Art* **1.14**
- Look, listen and make.
- Show your card.
- Rhyme: *Are you cold?* **2.13**

Unit 8 · Lesson 1

It's hot and sunny!

Key language:
What's the weather like?
(It's) sunny/cloudy.

- Warm up
- Hide and seek: *o, p* **2.17**
- Rhyme: *Are you cold?* **2.13**
- Look, listen and point. **2.18**
- Game: *What's the weather like?*
- Rhyme: *The sun has got his hat on!* **2.19**

a b c d e f g h i j k l m

Unit 8 • Lesson 2

It's cold and wet!

Key language:
Is the weather nice? wet; windy; bad

- Warm up
- Hide and seek: *q, r* **2.20**
- Rhyme: *Alphabet* [to *q, r*] **2.21**
- Look, listen and say. **2.22**
- Game: *It's hot!*
- Rhyme: *Incy Wincy spider* **2.23**

n o p q r s t u v w x y z

Unit 8 · Lesson 3

Count to 10

Key language:
ten; lunchbox; altogether; some

- Warm up
- Hide and seek: *10* **2.24**
- Rhyme: *Numbers* [to *10*] **2.25**
- Find and count: *10* **2.26**
- Game: *Bingo!*
- Rhyme: *Ten little children* **2.27**

10

0 1 2 3 4 5

Unit 8 • Lesson 4
All the same!

Key language:
(They are) all the same; hat

- Warm up
- Numbers: *0* to *10*
- Rhyme: *Numbers* [to *10*] **2.25**
- Find and count.
- Game: *All the same*
- Rhyme: *Ten little children* **2.27**

6 7 8 9 10

Unit 8 · Lesson 5
Hot and cold weather

Key language:
hot/cold drink; cold drink; soup

- Warm up
- Letters and numbers
- Rhyme: *Our world* **1.11**
- Listen and stick. **2.28–2.30**
- Game: *Weather bingo!*
- Rhyme: *Rain, rain go away!* **2.32**

1

2

Unit 8 • Lesson 6

Wet and dry

Key language:
dry; now; because

- Warm up
- Letters and numbers
- Rhyme: *Our world* 1.11
- Look and say.
- Game: *Weather*
- Rhyme: *The sun comes up.* 2.33

Unit 8 · Lesson 7

We need water

Key language:
water; turn the tap on/ off; Don't waste water

- Warm up
- Letters and numbers
- Rhyme: *Values* **1.13**
- Look, think and choose.
- Game: *What's the weather like?*
- Rhyme: *Goodbye* **1.5**

I turn the tap off.

Unit 8 • Lesson 8

Make a windsock

Key language:
windsock

- Warm up
- Letters and numbers
- Rhyme: *Art* 1.14
- Listen, look and make.
- Game: *Blowing in the wind.*
- Rhyme: *The sun comes up.* 2.33

1

2

3

4

Unit 9 • Lesson 1

Our pets

Key language: *What's that?; pet; rabbit; dog; teeth; claws; Don't touch! Be careful!*

- Warm up
- Hide and seek: *s, t* **2.34**
- Rhyme: *Alphabet* [to *s, t*] **2.35**
- Look, listen and say. **2.36**
- Game: *Who am I?*
- Rhyme: *Choose*

s t

a b c d e f g h i j k l m

Unit 9 · Lesson 2

Don't touch the fish!

Key language:
Don't hurt them!; They have ... ; very; feed

- Warm up
- Hide and seek: *u, v* **2.37**
- Rhyme: *Alphabet* [to *u, v*] **2.38**
- Look, listen and say. **2.39–2.40**
- Game: *Do/Don't ... !*
- Rhyme: *There are animals here.* **2.41**

u v

n o p q r s t u v w x y z

Unit 9 · Lesson 3

More and less

Key language:
one more; one less

- Warm up
- Numbers: *0* to *5*
- Rhyme: *One, two. How are you?* [to *10*] **2.42**
- Count and say.
- Game: *Make more, make less*
- Rhyme: *Five little cakes* **2.43**

0 1 2 3 4 5

Unit 9 • Lesson 4

Where's my teddy?

Key language:
under

- Warm up
- Numbers: *6* to *10*
- Rhyme: *Numbers* [to *10*] **2.25**
- Look, listen and stick. **2.44**
- Game: *Where?*
- Rhyme: *Where's my teddy?* **2.45**

6 7 8 9 10

Unit 9 • Lesson 5

Make small things big

Key language:
bird; bear; Make it look big; carefully

- Warm up
- Letters and numbers
- Rhyme: *Our world* 1.11
- Look, listen and point.
- Make it look big!
- Rhyme: *Goodbye* 1.5

Unit 9 · Lesson 6

Feathers, fur and scales

Key language:
fur; feathers; scales

- Warm up
- Letters and numbers
- Rhyme: *Our world* **1.11**
- Look, match and point. **2.46**
- Game: *Animals*
- Rhyme: *Shamlar the camel* **1.38**

Unit 9 • Lesson 7

Be kind to pets

Key language:
(Be) kind; Don't be (unkind).

- Warm up
- Letters and numbers
- Rhyme: *Values* **1.13**
- Look, think and draw.
- Game: *Kind to pets.*
- Rhyme: *Uncle Ali has a farm.* **1.69**

I am kind to pets.

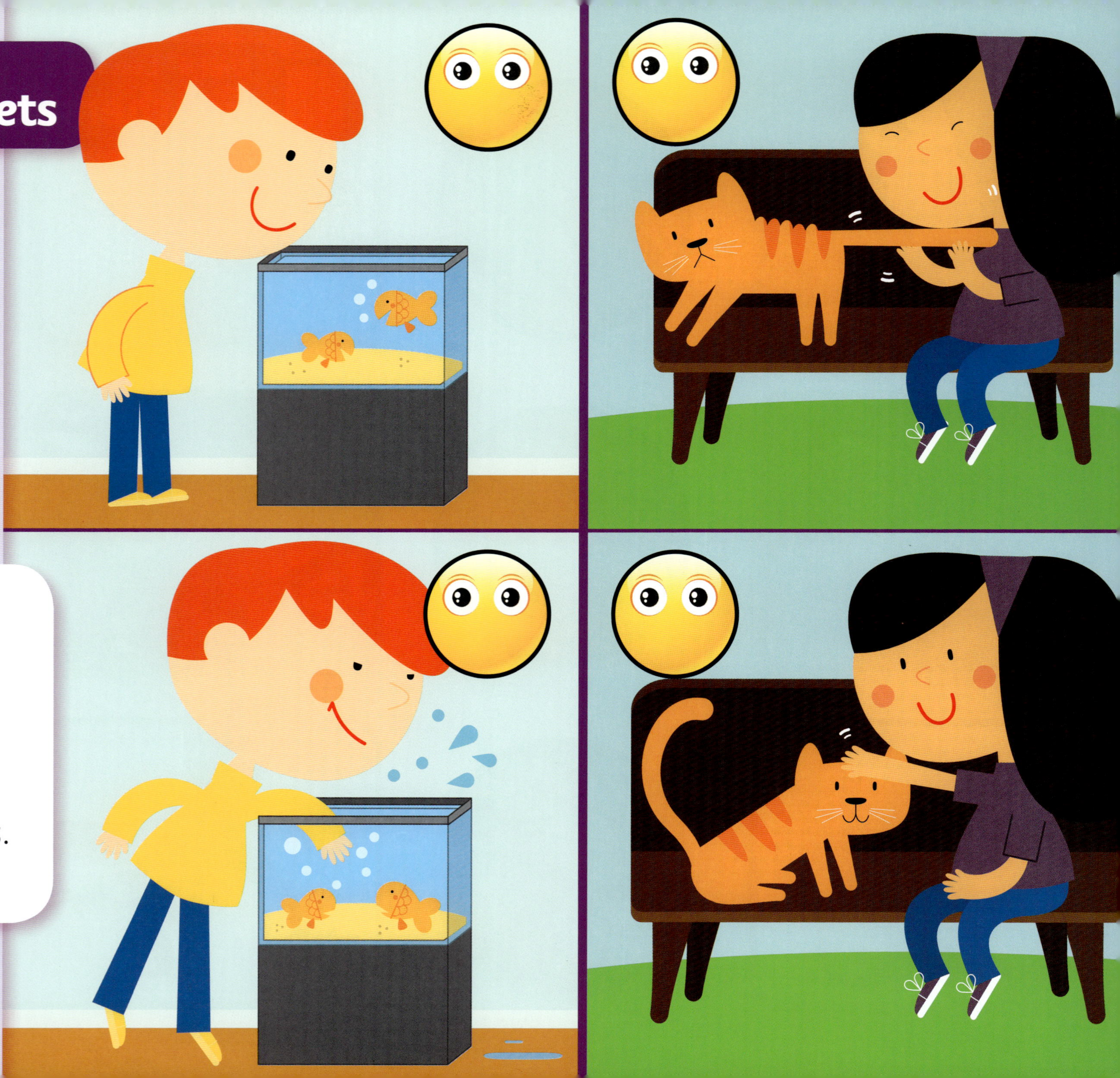

Unit 9 • Lesson 8

Paint a butterfly

1

2

Key language:
paint; half; both; leave to dry

- Warm up
- Letters and numbers
- Rhyme: *Art* 1.14
- Look, listen and make.
- Game: *Animal jigsaws*
- Rhyme: *I'm a butterfly!* 2.47

3

4

Unit 10 · Lesson 1

Day

Key language: *day; light; in school; night; dark; at home; Everyone is (asleep).*

- Warm up
- Hide and seek: *w, x* **2.48**
- Rhyme: *The sun has got his hat on!* **2.19**
- Listen, point and say. **2.49–2.50**
- Game: *Day or night?* **2.51**
- Rhyme: *Goodnight* **2.52**

w x

a b c d e f g h i j k l m

Unit 10 • Lesson 2

Night

Key language:
bright; moon; stars

- Warm up
- Hide and seek: *y, z* **2.53**
- Rhyme: *Goodnight* **2.52**
- Listen and stick. **2.54–2.55**
- Game: *Day and night*
- Rhyme: *Alphabet* [*a* to *z*] **2.56**

y z

n o p q r s t u v w x y z

Unit 10 • Lesson 3

Sharing

Key language:
skittles

- Warm up
- Rhyme: *Five baby ducks* **1.55**
- Hide and seek: *0* to *10*
- Listen and count. **2.57**
- Game: *Count together!*
- Rhyme: *One, two, three, four, five* **2.58**

0 1 2 3 4 5

Unit 10 • Lesson 4

Sharing pictures

Key language:
shape

- Warm up
- Numbers: *0* to *10*
- Rhyme: *Ten little children* **2.27**
- Listen and match. **2.59**
- Game: *Choose a shape.*
- Rhyme: *Numbers* [*1* to *10*] **2.25**

6 7 8 9 10

Unit 10 · Lesson 5

Rainbows

Key language:
rainbow; (It's) raining; rain; together

- Warm up
- Letters and numbers
- Rhyme: *Our world* 1.11
- Listen and circle. 2.60
- Game: *I can be a rainbow.*
- Rhyme: *The sun comes up.* (V1–2) 2.61

Unit 10 · Lesson 6
Shadows

Key language:
shadow; guess; move; change

- Warm up
- Letters and numbers
- Rhyme: *Our world* **1.11**
- Look and match.
- Game: *Shadow tag*
- Rhyme: *My shadow* **2.62**

Unit 10 • Lesson 7

Bedtime!

Key language:
bedtime; Go to bed; (Don't) make a fuss; naughty

- Warm up
- Letters and numbers
- Rhyme: *Values* **1.13**
- Listen, think and choose. **2.63**
- Game: *Choose*
- Rhyme: *Goodbye* **1.5**

I don't make a fuss at bedtime.

Unit 10 · Lesson 8

Starry night

Key language:
splash; stamp

- Warm up
- Letters and numbers
- Rhyme: *Art* 1.14
- Look, listen and make.
- Game: *Day and night*
- Rhyme: *Twinkle, twinkle, little star!* 2.64

1

2

3

4

aA bB cC dD eE

kK lL mM nN

sS tT uU vV

fF gG hH iI jJ

oO pP qQ rR

wW xX yY zZ

0 1 2

6 7 8

3

4

5

9

10

CENGAGE Learning

Hide and Seek Pupil's Book 1, 1st Edition

Jane Thompson and Stephen Thompson

Publisher: Sharon Jervis

Commissioning Editor: Carol Goodwright

Development Editor: Carol Goodwright

Content Project Manager: Jon Ricketts

Manufacturing Buyer: Eyvett Davis

Head of Strategic Marketing – ELT: Charlotte Ellis

Design and Composition: Tighe | SPi Global

The authors and publisher would like to thank the following for their collaboration in this project:

Consultants and Readers:
Jennifer Heath, ELT author and consultant, Europe; David A. Hill, ELT author and consultant, Europe; Luciana Verónica Fernández, Early Literacy Specialist and Teacher Trainer, Argentina; Tom Kelley, Educational Consultant, Cengage Learning, UAE; Sandra Zahar, Kindergarten Teacher, UAE; Sondos Fakhr El Deen, Teacher, Egypt; Yuta Otake, Kindergarten Teacher and Specialist, U.S.A; Honny Steward, Director, Global Books, Indonesia; Doris Au, Hong Kong , Stella Zhu, Center Director, Better English, China; Delila Saskia, Indonesia

Illustrators:
4-8, 12-15, 17 stickers, 20-23, 28-31, 36-39, 44-47, 52-55, 60-63, 68-71, 76-79 Nathan Jarvis; 10, 26, 34, 42, 49-50, 58, 74, 82 Steve Mack

Recordings: Recorded in London by John Green TEFL Audio. Music for the songs and chants composed and arranged by Tim Woolf.

Commissioned photos: Martyn F. Chillmaid

Photo Credit: All images sourced from Shutterstock unless otherwise stated:
8 (l) Jaimie Duplass; **8 (r)** Ami Parikh; **9 (l)** Markiss; **9 (r)** Blend Images; **9 (bkgd)** Elenamiv; **16 (t, c)** Kruglov Orda; **16 (bl, bc, cr)** LehaKoK; **16 (tr, br)** Ng Wei Keong; **17 (tr)** Eric Isselee; **17 (br)** Sergey Novikov; **17 (tr bkgd)** Photolinc; **17 (tl)** Natursports; **17 (bl)** Christopher Meder; **18 (tl)** StudioVin; **18 (tr)** De Visu; **18 (bl)** Poznyakov; **18 (br)** Paul Vasarhelyi; **24 (c)** Andrey Burmakin; **24 (r)** Jaroslava V; **24 (tl)** Kesu; **24 (br)** DenisNata; **25 (tl)** Prapass; **25 (bl)** Eric Isselee; **25 (br)** Aaron Amat; **25 (tc)** Wirat Pangprasert; **25 (cr)** JDCarballo; **32 (ct)** Jang14; **32 (tr)** Gemmy; **32 (bl)** Wendy Nero; **32 (br)** Filip Fuxa; **32 (tl)** Andrew Burgess; **32 (bc)** Kosin Sukhum; **32 (cb)** Eric Isselee; **32 (tc)** Nicole Sharp; **33 (tl)** Petrenko Andriy; **33 (bl)** XiXinXing; **33 (r)** Rahhal; **34, 42, 58, 74, 82 (yellow face)** Kostenyukova Nataliya; **40 (cl)** Fotografas Edgaras; **40 (cr)** Nenov Brothers Images; **40 (tl)** Bar 2; **40 (tc)** HSNphotography; **40 (bc)** mistery; **40 (bl)** StudioSmart; **40 (br)** AXL; **40 (tr)** Twin Design; **41 (tl)** iStock.com/Eric Isselee; **41 (br)** JeniFoto; **41 (bl)** Stockbyte/Getty Images; **41 (tr)** Michel Borges; **41 (bc)** Eric Isselee; **41 (cl)** AGorohov; **48 (bl)** Alexander Raths; **48 (tl)** Dmitry Kalinovsky; **48 (bc)** Drago Nika; **48 (tr)** DenisNata; **48 (br)** Utekhina Anna; **48 (tr bkgd)** Robert S; **48 (br bkgd)** Yellowj; **56 (tl)** Sergiy Kuzmin; **56 (tlb)** Artville; **56 (tr)** Svetlana Lukienko; **56 (cl)** Sukharevskyy Dmytro; **56 (bl)** Andrey Armyagov; **56 (br)** Ewa Studio; **56 (cr)** Nitr; **56 (tc)** TatjanaRittner; **56 (bc)** Kunkie99; **64 (l)** Warren Goldswain; **64 (r)** Mandy Godbehear; **64 (r bkgd)** Creative Travel Projects; **65 (bkgd)** Paprika; **65 (tlbkgd)** TyBy; **65 (c)** SlipFloat; **65 (bl)** Janis Smits; **65 (tl)** Alexey Losevich; **65 (tr)** lumen-digital; **65 (br)** Sandra van der Steen; **72 (tc)** Critterbiz; **72 (br)** Randy Yarbrough; **72 (br inset)** Anton Derevschuk; **72 (bl)** Shutterstock; **72 (magnifying glass)** Pixotico; **73 (tc)** Microstock Man; **73 (c)** Mikhail Klyoshev; **73 (bc)** Sayanjo65; **73 (tl)** Kamonrat; **73 (cl)** Radka Palenikova; **73 (bl)** Jiang Hongyan; **73 (tr)** Dmitry Kalinovsky; **73 (cr)** StevenRussellSmithPhotos; **73 (br)** ArunRoisri; **80 (c)** luchschen; **80 (b)** Kirbyedy; **81 (c)** Cengage.

Sticker Photo Credits:
9 Monkey Business Images/Shutterstock; **Smiley face:** Patimat Alieva/Shutterstock; **18** 3445128471/Shutterstock; **25 (feather)** MustafaNC/Shutterstock; **25 (weight)** Mrs ya/Shutterstock; **64 (ice cream)** Enrico Jose/Shutterstock; **64 (orange juice)** M. Unal Ozmen/Shutterstock; **64 (tea)** Suslik1983/Shutterstock; **64 (soup)** Teresa Kasprzycka/Shutterstock.

British Library Cataloguing-in-Publication Data
A catalogue record for this book is available from the British Library.

ISBN: 9781408062166

Cengage Learning EMEA
Cheriton House, North Way, Andover, Hampshire, SP10 5BE United Kingdom

Cengage Learning products are represented in Canada by Nelson Education Ltd.

For your lifelong learning solutions, visit **www.cengage.co.uk**

Printed in China by RR Donnelley
Print Number 01 Print Year 2014

Unit 1

Unit 2

Unit 3

Unit 6, page 46

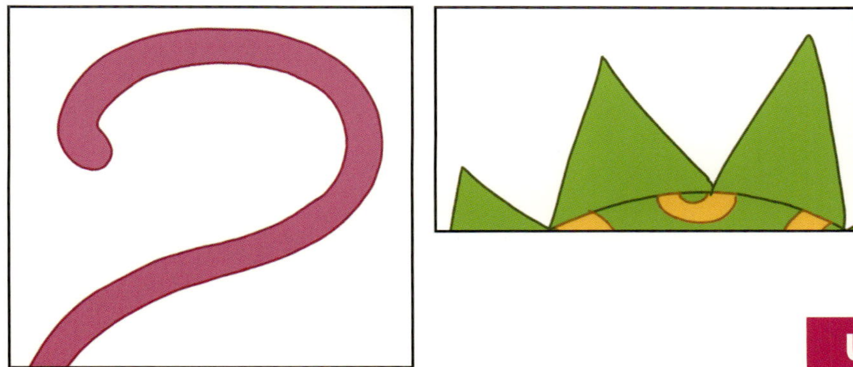

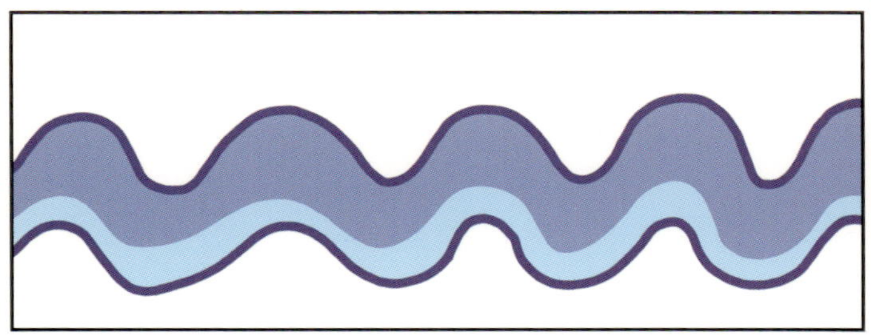

Unit 5

Unit 6, page 47

Unit 7

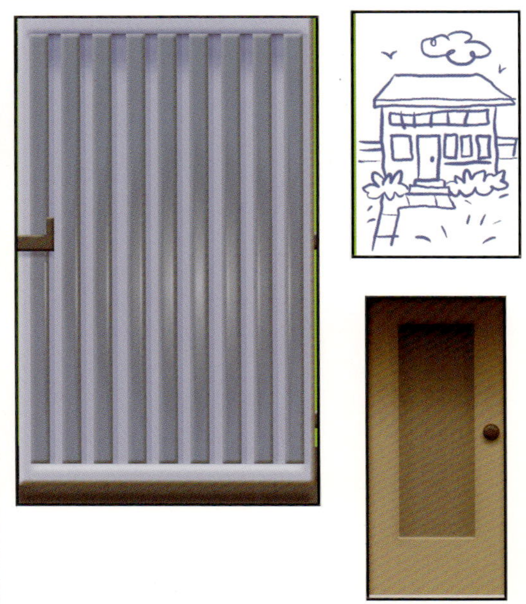

Unit 8

Unit 9

Self-assessment stickers

Unit 10, page 76

Unit 10, page 77

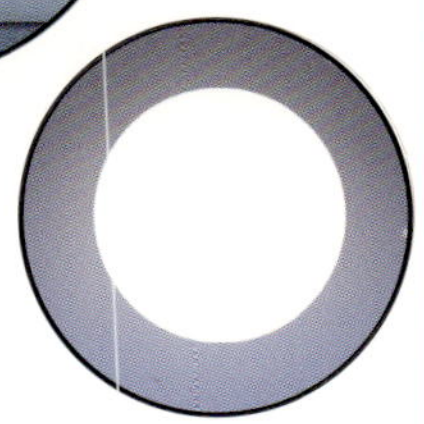

Unit 10, page 81

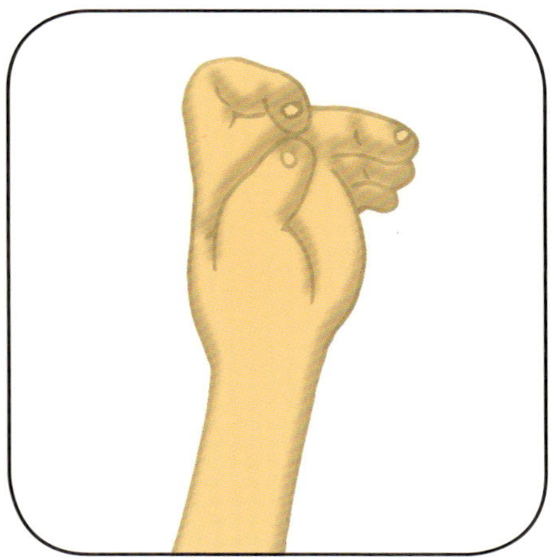

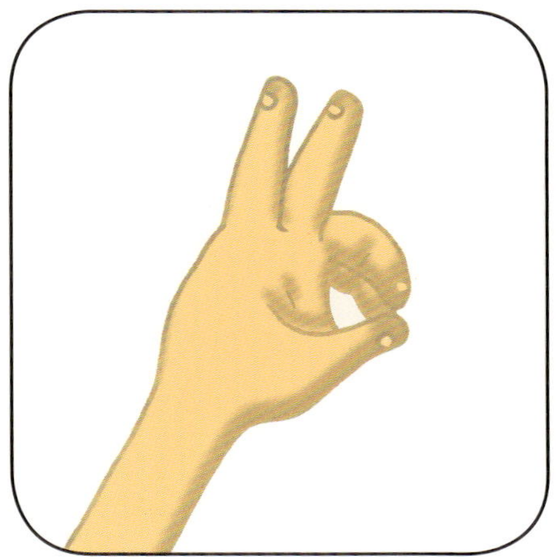